BELLS/GLOCKENSPIEL
101 DISNEY SONGS

Available for
FLUTE, CLARINET, ALTO SAX, TENOR SAX, TRUMPET,
HORN, TROMBONE, VIOLIN, VIOLA, CELLO, RECORDER,
BELLS/GLOCKENSPIEL

ISBN 978-1-7051-3864-9

The following songs are the property of:

Bourne Co.
Music Publishers
5 West 37th Street
New York, NY 10018

BABY MINE
GIVE A LITTLE WHISTLE
HEIGH-HO
HI-DIDDLE-DEE-DEE (AN ACTOR'S LIFE FOR ME)
I'M WISHING
I'VE GOT NO STRINGS
SOME DAY MY PRINCE WILL COME
WHEN I SEE AN ELEPHANT FLY
WHEN YOU WISH UPON A STAR
WHISTLE WHILE YOU WORK
WHO'S AFRAID OF THE BIG BAD WOLF?
WITH A SMILE AND A SONG

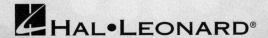

Visit Hal Leonard Online at
www.halleonard.com

Contact us:
Hal Leonard
7777 West Bluemound Road
Milwaukee, WI 53213
Email: info@halleonard.com

In Europe, contact:
Hal Leonard Europe Limited
42 Wigmore Street
Marylebone, London, W1U 2RN
Email: info@halleonardeurope.com

In Australia, contact:
Hal Leonard Australia Pty. Ltd.
4 Lentara Court
Cheltenham, Victoria, 3192 Australia
Email: info@halleonard.com.au

CONTENTS

*Based on the "Winnie the Pooh" works,
by A. A. Milne and E. H. Shepard

**TARZAN® Owned by Edgar Rice Burroughs, Inc.
and Used by Permission.
© Burroughs/Disney

BABY MINE
from DUMBO

Words by NED WASHINGTON
Music by FRANK CHURCHILL

THE BALLAD OF DAVY CROCKETT
from DAVY CROCKETT

Words by TOM BLACKBURN
Music by GEORGE BRUNS

BELLA NOTTE
from LADY AND THE TRAMP

Music and Lyrics by PEGGY LEE
and SONNY BURKE

BE OUR GUEST
from BEAUTY AND THE BEAST

BELLS

Lyrics by HOWARD ASHMAN
Music by ALAN MENKEN

BEAUTY AND THE BEAST
from BEAUTY AND THE BEAST

Bells

Lyrics by HOWARD ASHMAN
Music by ALAN MENKEN

Moderately slow

BELLE
from BEAUTY AND THE BEAST

BELLS

Music by ALAN MENKEN
Lyrics by HOWARD ASHMAN

BIBBIDI-BOBBIDI-BOO
(The Magic Song)
from CINDERELLA

Words by JERRY LIVINGSTON
Music by MACK DAVID and AL HOFFMAN

Brightly

BREAKING FREE
from HIGH SCHOOL MUSICAL

BELLS

Words and Music by
JAMIE HOUSTON

BEST OF FRIENDS
from THE FOX AND THE HOUND

Bells

Words by STAN FIDEL
Music by RICHARD JOHNSTON

CAN YOU FEEL THE LOVE TONIGHT
from THE LION KING

BELLS

Music by ELTON JOHN
Lyrics by TIM RICE

Pop Ballad

CANDLE ON THE WATER

from PETE'S DRAGON

Bells

Words and Music by AL KASHA
and JOEL HIRSCHHORN

Spiritually

CHIM CHIM CHER-EE

from MARY POPPINS

BELLS

Words and Music by RICHARD M. SHERMAN
and ROBERT B. SHERMAN

Lightly, with gusto

small notes optional

CIRCLE OF LIFE
from THE LION KING

BELLS

Music by ELTON JOHN
Lyrics by TIM RICE

Moderately (with an African beat)

THE CLIMB
from HANNAH MONTANA: THE MOVIE

BELLS

Words and Music by JESSI ALEXANDER
and JON MABE

BELLS

CRUELLA DE VIL
from 101 DALMATIANS

Words and Music by
MEL LEVEN

A DREAM IS A WISH YOUR HEART MAKES
from CINDERELLA

Words and Music by MACK DAVID,
AL HOFFMAN and JERRY LIVINGSTON

FEED THE BIRDS
(Tuppence a Bag)
from MARY POPPINS

Words and Music by RICHARD M. SHERMAN
and ROBERT B. SHERMAN

COLORS OF THE WIND
from POCAHONTAS

BELLS

Music by ALAN MENKEN
Lyrics by STEPHEN SCHWARTZ

DO YOU WANT TO BUILD A SNOWMAN?

from FROZEN

BELLS

Music and Lyrics by KRISTEN ANDERSON-LOPEZ
and ROBERT LOPEZ

DAYS IN THE SUN
from BEAUTY AND THE BEAST

BELLS

Music by ALAN MENKEN
Lyrics by TIM RICE

EVERMORE
from BEAUTY AND THE BEAST

BELLS

Music by ALAN MENKEN
Lyrics by TIM RICE

HEIGH-HO
(The Dwarfs' Marching Song)
from SNOW WHITE AND THE SEVEN DWARFS

Words by LARRY MOREY
Music by FRANK CHURCHILL

Brightly, cheerfully

FOR THE FIRST TIME IN FOREVER

from FROZEN

BELLS

Music and Lyrics by KRISTEN ANDERSON-LOPEZ
and ROBERT LOPEZ

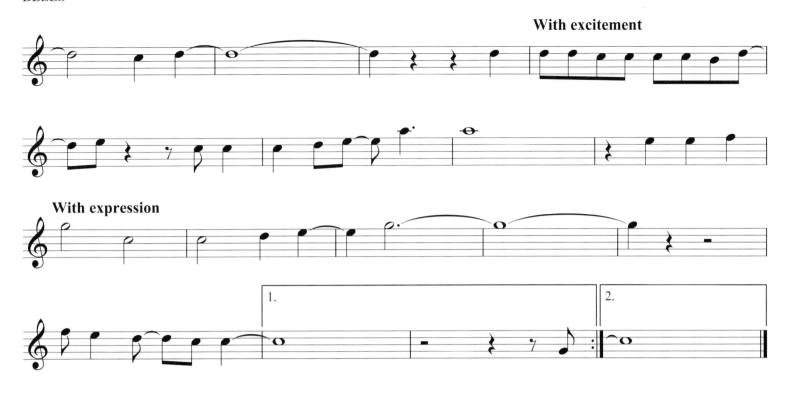

HI-DIDDLE-DEE-DEE
(An Actor's Life for Me)
from PINOCCHIO

Words by NED WASHINGTON
Music by LEIGH HARLINE

FRIEND LIKE ME

from ALADDIN

BELLS

Lyrics by HOWARD ASHMAN
Music by ALAN MENKEN

GASTON
from BEAUTY AND THE BEAST

BELLS

Music by ALAN MENKEN
Lyrics by HOWARD ASHMAN

Moderately slow, in 1

GOD HELP THE OUTCASTS

from THE HUNCHBACK OF NOTRE DAME

Bells

Music by ALAN MENKEN
Lyrics by STEPHEN SCHWARTZ

GIVE A LITTLE WHISTLE

from PINOCCHIO

Words by NED WASHINGTON
Music by LEIGH HARLINE

Moderately, in 2

GO THE DISTANCE

from HERCULES

BELLS

Music by ALAN MENKEN
Lyrics by DAVID ZIPPEL

HAKUNA MATATA

from THE LION KING

BELLS

Music by ELTON JOHN
Lyrics by TIM RICE

HAPPY WORKING SONG

from ENCHANTED

BELLS

Music by ALAN MENKEN
Lyrics by STEPHEN SCHWARTZ

HE'S A PIRATE

from PIRATES OF THE CARIBBEAN: THE CURSE OF THE BLACK PEARL

BELLS

Music by KLAUS BADELT,
GEOFFREY ZANELLI and HANS ZIMMER

HE'S A TRAMP
from LADY AND THE TRAMP

Words and Music by PEGGY LEE
and SONNY BURKE

Moderately

HOW DOES A MOMENT LAST FOREVER

from BEAUTY AND THE BEAST

BELLS

Music by ALAN MENKEN
Lyrics by TIM RICE

I JUST CAN'T WAIT TO BE KING

from THE LION KING

BELLS

Music by ELTON JOHN
Lyrics by TIM RICE

Bright Two-beat

HOW FAR I'LL GO

from MOANA

BELLS

Music and Lyrics by
LIN-MANUEL MIRANDA

Moderately, in 2

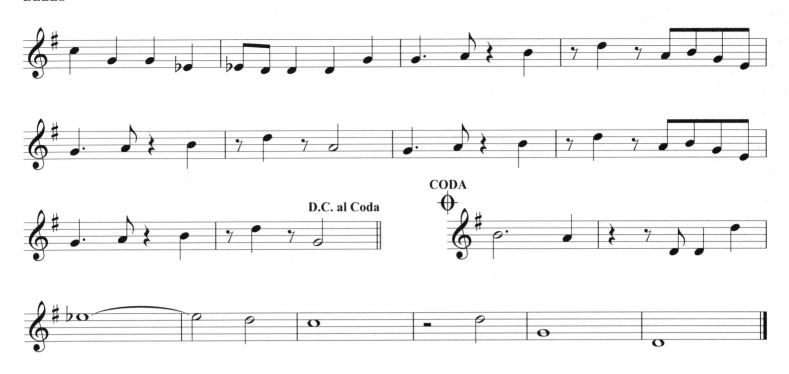

I'M LATE
from ALICE IN WONDERLAND

Words by BOB HILLIARD
Music by SAMMY FAIN

Moderately fast

I SEE THE LIGHT

from TANGLED

BELLS

Music by ALAN MENKEN
Lyrics by GLENN SLATER

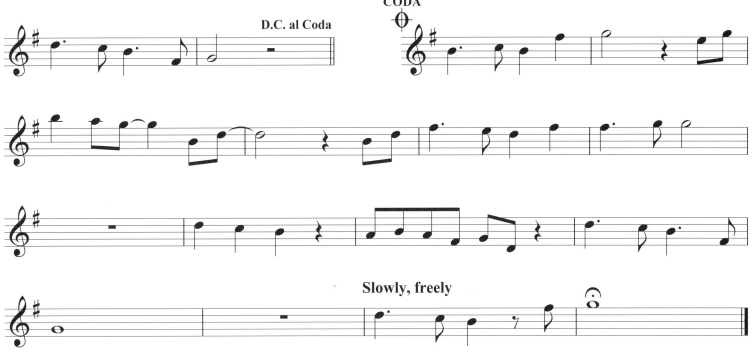

I'M WISHING
from SNOW WHITE AND THE SEVEN DWARFS

Words by LARRY MOREY
Music by FRANK CHURCHILL

I'LL MAKE A MAN OUT OF YOU
from MULAN

BELLS

Music by MATTHEW WILDER
Lyrics by DAVID ZIPPEL

IN SUMMER
from FROZEN

BELLS

Music and Lyrics by KRISTEN ANDERSON-LOPEZ
and ROBERT LOPEZ

Moderately, in 2

I'VE GOT A DREAM

from TANGLED

BELLS

Music by ALAN MENKEN
Lyrics by GLENN SLATER

Moderately fast

IF I CAN'T LOVE HER
from BEAUTY AND THE BEAST: THE BROADWAY MUSICAL

BELLS

Music by ALAN MENKEN
Lyrics by TIM RICE

IF I NEVER KNEW YOU

(End Title)

from POCAHONTAS

BELLS

Music by ALAN MENKEN
Lyrics by STEPHEN SCHWARTZ

Moderately slow

I'VE GOT NO STRINGS
from PINOCCHIO

BELLS

Words by NED WASHINGTON
Music by LEIGH HARLINE

IT'S A SMALL WORLD
from Disney Parks' "it's a small world" attraction

Words and Music by RICHARD M. SHERMAN
and ROBERT B. SHERMAN

KISS THE GIRL

from THE LITTLE MERMAID

Music by ALAN MENKEN
Lyrics by HOWARD ASHMAN

BELLS

LAVA
from LAVA

BELLS

Music and Lyrics by
JAMES FORD MURPHY

Moderately slow, in 2

LOVE IS AN OPEN DOOR

from FROZEN

BELLS

Music and Lyrics by KRISTEN ANDERSON-LOPEZ
and ROBERT LOPEZ

LET IT GO
from FROZEN

BELLS

Music and Lyrics by KRISTEN ANDERSON-LOPEZ
and ROBERT LOPEZ

Slowly, in 2

LAVENDER BLUE
(Dilly Dilly)
from SO DEAR TO MY HEART

BELLS

Words by LARRY MOREY
Music by ELIOT DANIEL

MICKEY MOUSE MARCH
from THE MICKEY MOUSE CLUB

Words and Music by
JIMMIE DODD

LET'S GO FLY A KITE

from MARY POPPINS

Words and Music by RICHARD M. SHERMAN
and ROBERT B. SHERMAN

With gusto

THE LORD IS GOOD TO ME
from MELODY TIME

BELLS

Words and Music by KIM GANNON
and WALTER KENT

MY FUNNY FRIEND AND ME
from THE EMPEROR'S NEW GROOVE

Lyrics by STING
Music by STING and DAVID HARTLEY

PART OF YOUR WORLD

from THE LITTLE MERMAID

Bells

Music by ALAN MENKEN
Lyrics by HOWARD ASHMAN

Moderately bright

MOTHER KNOWS BEST

from TANGLED

BELLS

Music by ALAN MENKEN
Lyrics by GLENN SLATER

Moderately slow, in 2

A PIRATE'S LIFE

from PETER PAN

Words by ED PENNER
Music by OLIVER WALLACE

Moderately, with a bounce

RUMBLY IN MY TUMBLY

from THE MANY ADVENTURES OF WINNIE THE POOH

Words and Music by RICHARD M. SHERMAN
and ROBERT B. SHERMAN

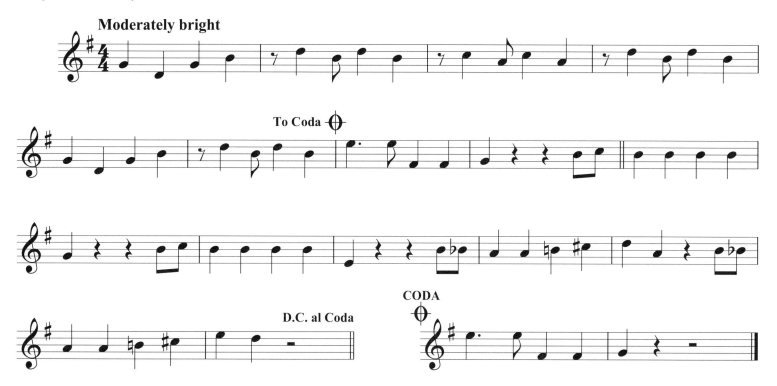

REFLECTION
from MULAN

BELLS

Music by MATTHEW WILDER
Lyrics by DAVID ZIPPEL

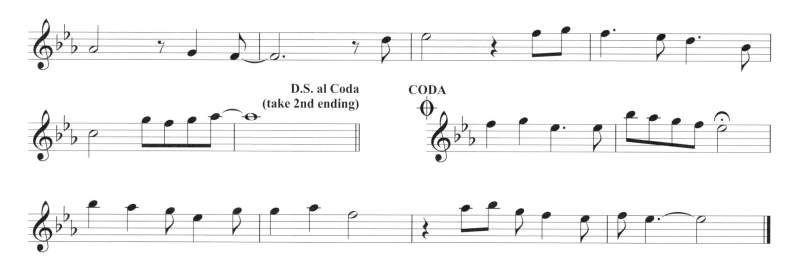

THE SECOND STAR TO THE RIGHT

from PETER PAN

Words by SAMMY CAHN
Music by SAMMY FAIN

SEIZE THE DAY
from NEWSIES

BELLS

Music by ALAN MENKEN
Lyrics by JACK FELDMAN

SO THIS IS LOVE
(The Cinderella Waltz)
from CINDERELLA

BELLS

Words and Music by MACK DAVID,
AL HOFFMAN and JERRY LIVINGSTON

Moderately

SO CLOSE
from ENCHANTED

BELLS

Music by ALAN MENKEN
Lyrics by STEPHEN SCHWARTZ

Moderately slow, in 4

THE SIAMESE CAT SONG
from LADY AND THE TRAMP

BELLS

Words and Music by PEGGY LEE
and SONNY BURKE

SOME DAY MY PRINCE WILL COME
from SNOW WHITE AND THE SEVEN DWARFS

Words by LARRY MOREY
Music by FRANK CHURCHILL

SOMEDAY
from THE HUNCHBACK OF NOTRE DAME

Music by ALAN MENKEN
Lyrics by STEPHEN SCHWARTZ

Bells

SOMETHING THERE

from BEAUTY AND THE BEAST

Bells

Music by ALAN MENKEN
Lyrics by HOWARD ASHMAN

Moderately fast

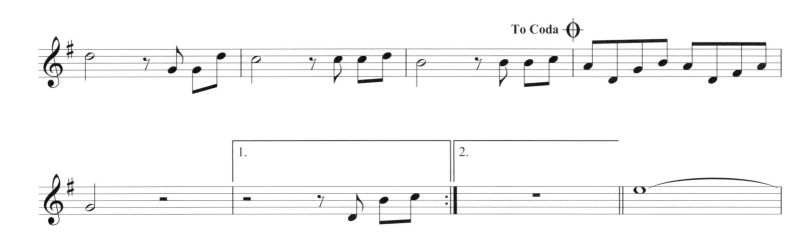

A SPOONFUL OF SUGAR

from MARY POPPINS

Bells

Words and Music by RICHARD M. SHERMAN
and ROBERT B. SHERMAN

SUPERCALIFRAGILISTICEXPIALIDOCIOUS

from MARY POPPINS

BELLS

Words and Music by RICHARD M. SHERMAN
and ROBERT B. SHERMAN

Brightly

"THIS IS ME."
from RATATOUILLE

BELLS

Music by MICHAEL GIACCHINO

THAT'S HOW YOU KNOW
from ENCHANTED

BELLS

Music by ALAN MENKEN
Lyrics by STEPHEN SCHWARTZ

TOYLAND MARCH
from BABES IN TOYLAND

Adapted from V. HERBERT Melody
Words by MEL LEVEN
Music by GEORGE BRUNS

March tempo

TRASHIN' THE CAMP
(Pop Version)
from TARZAN™

BELLS

Words and Music by
PHIL COLLINS

THE UNBIRTHDAY SONG
from ALICE IN WONDERLAND

Bells

Words and Music by MACK DAVID,
AL HOFFMAN and JERRY LIVINGSTON

TRUE LOVE'S KISS

from ENCHANTED

BELLS

Music by ALAN MENKEN
Lyrics by STEPHEN SCHWARTZ

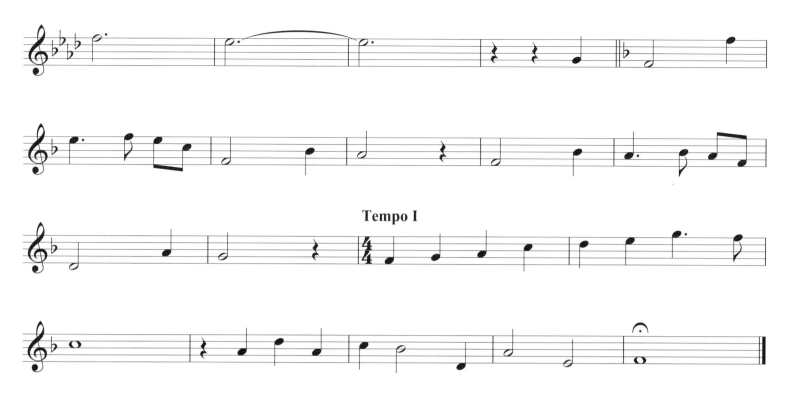

Tempo I

WESTWARD HO, THE WAGONS!
from WESTWARD HO, THE WAGONS!

Words by TOM BLACKBURN
Music by GEORGE BRUNS

Lively

WE BELONG TOGETHER

from TOY STORY 3

BELLS

Music and Lyrics by
RANDY NEWMAN

WHEN I SEE AN ELEPHANT FLY

from DUMBO

Words by NED WASHINGTON
Music by OLIVER WALLACE

WE KNOW THE WAY

from MOANA

BELLS

Music by OPETAIA FOA'I
Lyrics by OPETAIA FOA'I
and LIN-MANUEL MIRANDA

A WHALE OF A TALE
from 20,000 LEAGUES UNDER THE SEA

Bells

Words and Music by NORMAN GIMBEL
and AL HOFFMAN

WE'RE ALL IN THIS TOGETHER

from HIGH SCHOOL MUSICAL

Bells

Words and Music by MATTHEW GERRARD
and ROBBIE NEVIL

WHISTLE WHILE YOU WORK
from SNOW WHITE AND THE SEVEN DWARFS

Words by LARRY MOREY
Music by FRANK CHURCHILL

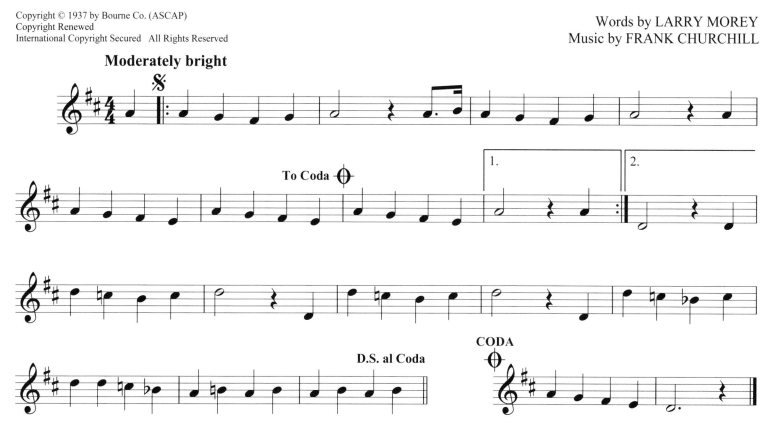

WHEN SHE LOVED ME
from TOY STORY 2

BELLS

Music and Lyrics by
RANDY NEWMAN

Tenderly, very freely

WHEN YOU WISH UPON A STAR

from PINOCCHIO

BELLS

Words by NED WASHINGTON
Music by LEIGH HARLINE

Moderately

WHEN WILL MY LIFE BEGIN?

from TANGLED

BELLS

Music by ALAN MENKEN
Lyrics by GLENN SLATER

WITH A SMILE AND A SONG
from SNOW WHITE AND THE SEVEN DWARFS

Words by LARRY MOREY
Music by FRANK CHURCHILL

WHO'S AFRAID OF THE BIG BAD WOLF?

from THREE LITTLE PIGS

BELLS

Words and Music by
FRANK CHURCHILL
Additional Lyric by ANN RONELL

Moderately, in 2

WINNIE THE POOH
from THE MANY ADVENTURES OF WINNIE THE POOH

Words and Music by RICHARD M. SHERMAN
and ROBERT B. SHERMAN

Bells

A WHOLE NEW WORLD
from ALADDIN

BELLS

Music by ALAN MENKEN
Lyrics by TIM RICE

THE WONDERFUL THING ABOUT TIGGERS

from THE MANY ADVENTURES OF WINNIE THE POOH

BELLS

Words and Music by RICHARD M. SHERMAN
and ROBERT B. SHERMAN

Very brightly

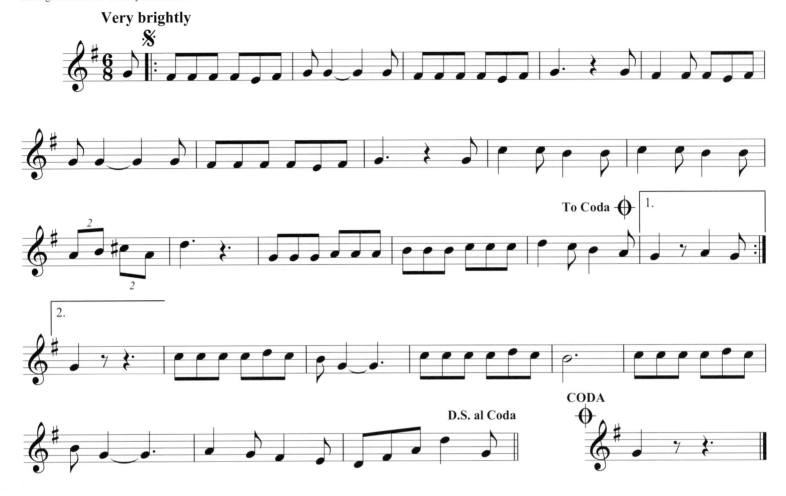

YO HO
(A Pirate's Life for Me)

from Disney Parks' Pirates of the Caribbean attraction

Words by XAVIER ATENCIO
Music by GEORGE BRUNS

In a robust manner

THEME FROM ZORRO
from the Television Series

Words by NORMAN FOSTER
Music by GEORGE BRUNS

Moderately, in 2

WRITTEN IN THE STARS

from AIDA

BELLS

Music by ELTON JOHN
Lyrics by TIM RICE

Slowly

YOU CAN FLY! YOU CAN FLY! YOU CAN FLY!

BELLS

from PETER PAN

Words by SAMMY CAHN
Music by SAMMY FAIN

Lively

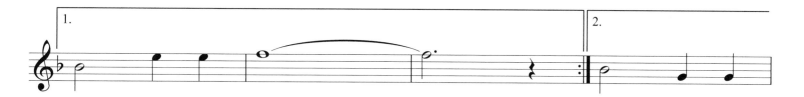

YOU ARE THE MUSIC IN ME

from HIGH SCHOOL MUSICAL 2

BELLS

Words and Music by
JAMIE HOUSTON

Moderately fast Rock

YOU'LL BE IN MY HEART

(Pop Version)

from Walt Disney Pictures' TARZAN™

Words and Music by
PHIL COLLINS

BELLS

YOU'RE WELCOME

from MOANA

BELLS

Music and Lyrics by
LIN-MANUEL MIRANDA

ZIP-A-DEE-DOO-DAH
from SONG OF THE SOUTH

Words by RAY GILBERT
Music by ALLIE WRUBEL

ZERO TO HERO
from HERCULES

BELLS

Music by ALAN MENKEN
Lyrics by DAVID ZIPPEL

YOU'VE GOT A FRIEND IN ME

from TOY STORY

BELLS

Music and Lyrics by
RANDY NEWMAN